New York

Places to Find
Peace and Quiet

Fifth Edition

Allan Ishac

Universe • New York

Acknowledgments

There are plenty of big boisterous books out there demanding to get a publisher's attention. This is a quiet little book that might have gotten overlooked if it hadn't been for the sensitivity of my editors, Kathleen Jayes, Caitlin Leffel, and Jacob Lehman, at Rizzoli/Universe. They have been the guardians of this guidebook and champions of its message for years, keeping it fresh, vital, and successfully in print through the last three editions. For that, I am grateful. I also want to thank Helene Silver, formerly of City and Company, who was the first to publish niche books like this one, focused specifically on New York. Finally, I appreciate the contributions of Bill Fitzhugh, Helen Maier, Barbara Moore, Amanda Rubin, Ouisie Shapiro, Richard Siegel, and other enthusiastic New Yorkers who generously offered their location ideas and support. Thank you all for valuing serene and silent places as much as I do.

First Universe edition published in the United States of America in 2003
by UNIVERSE PUBLISHING
a Division of Rizzoli International Publications, Inc.
300 Park Avenue South
New York, NY 10010

© 1991, 1995, 1997, 2001, 2003, 2004, 2007 by Allan Ishac
Previously published by City and Company
Interior Design by Don Wise & Co., based on an original design by Nancy Steiny
Cover Design: Paul Kepple and Jude Buffum @ Headcase Design
Cover Illustration by Mary Lynn Blasutta
Typesetting by Tina Henderson

2007 2008 2009 2010 / 10 9 8 7 6 5 4 3 2 1
Fifth Edition
Printed in the United States
Library of Congress Catalog Control Number: 2007903835
ISBN 13: 978-0-7893-1575-5

Publisher's Note: Neither Universe Publishing nor the author has any interest, financial or personal, in the locations listed in this book. While every effort was made to ensure that all data was accurate at the time of publication, we advise calling ahead or checking Web sites to confirm details.

Dedication

I love New Yorkers. They put up with an amazing amount of inconvenience and annoyances every day, and they still play nice. They face endless challenges living in a demanding metropolis, and still keep smiling. I give this book to them, in the hope that peaceful sanctuaries, serene retreats, and tranquil escapes can make their days go just a bit easier. Rest a while, friends.

Contents

Preface

In the summer of 2003, on a steamy afternoon in August, the power went out in New York City. Off went the lights, the network computers, the air-conditioning systems. The subways stopped, and with no traffic signals, cars came to a halt. Eventually, the juice ran out on cell phones and Blackberries and iPods, and they shut down, too.

As night fell, and there was still no electricity, the city slowly went black. Then it became remarkably silent. Without the constant thrum of rooftop HVAC units, the sonic chaos of traffic horns, and the subterranean rumble of the trains—noxious intrusions we seem barely to notice as we race through our days—the city turned quiet in a way I've never heard before.

I was delighted.

Of course, I'm someone who craves peace and quiet. I also believe that a daily dose of both are essential to good health and sustained happiness. Studies as far back as 1975 have concluded that excessive noise contributes to high blood pressure, fatigue, increased anxiety, and difficulty concentrating. Noise, the number one quality-of-life complaint on the city's 311 hotline—and more ubiquitous than any other pollution we face—is making us tired, irritable, even ill.

Politically minded folks would advocate pressuring our elected officials to put more teeth into the city's noise code (a 2006 revision of the code has come under fire by critics who say it did not go far enough). I'd simply ask the mayor to shut the power off occasionally.

In the meantime, we can all honk and holler less, walk and whisper more, and increase the peace any way we can. Keeping an eye on our own "noise footprint" will result in a quieter, more serene, and ultimately more people-friendly New York.

Allan Ishac

Introduction

Peace and quiet are not the first words
that come to mind when you think of
New York. The world's greatest city can
also be a hard-driving place, operating at
maximum volume and demanding that
we be in constant motion. Since 9/11,
hovering threat levels and the fears
they engender have also added to
our tensions.

You can't count on finding solitude and
serenity at home, either. With yelping
dogs, blaring car alarms, and grinding
garbage trucks right outside our
windows, many of us keep the earplugs
by the night table and postpone real rest
and relaxation for vacation time.

That's why I believe we need access to
urban sanctuaries as never before.
Unfortunately, locations offering peace
and quiet are becoming more rare just as
they are more needed. The economic
realities of New York work against
landlords and building owners setting
aside valuable real estate for solace
and refuge.

That's where this little book comes in. For more than fifteen years and through five editions, it has been a reliable guide to tranquil, stress-free zones that provide a gentle counterbalance to the noise, fast pace, and high-tech distractions that pull at us every day. It offers a way to leave the city behind without ever leaving the city.

I've included havens and hideaways in all five boroughs—some outside, some indoors, some that charge a fee, and many that are free. These are safe, serene retreats that will allow you to decompress from city stress and surround yourself in solitude.

Of course, the need to escape to a tranquil place can strike suddenly and insistently, and when the soul craves silence, it is best to listen. Keep this book close at hand—the perfect place is just a page or two away.

Astor Court
at the Met

Address: Metropolitan Museum of Art,
Fifth Ave. and 82nd St.
Phone: (212) 535-7710
Hours: Tuesday through Thursday, Sunday,
9:30 A.M. to 5:30 P.M.; Friday and Saturday,
9:30 A.M. to 9 P.M.; closed Monday
Admission: $20 suggested donation
Subway: 4, 5, 6 to 86th St., walk west
Bus: M1, 2, 3, 4, 5 to 82nd St.
Website: www.metmuseum.org

brooke Astor, one of the city's great philan-

thropists, spent part of her childhood in Beijing.

Cherished memories of her time there inspired

her to conceive and fund a Chinese garden at

the Metropolitan Museum of Art in 1981.

Astor Court is a flawlessly recreated

Ming Dynasty scholar's garden, modeled after

an existing courtyard in the city of Suzhou.

It is an unspoken rule of the Met that this refined

environment retains its sanctuarylike qualities.

Thus, voices are lowered, cameras are pocketed,

and visitors wander the pillared walkways in a state of reverie and respect.

Meant for contemplation of nature, the courtyard contains a rock garden, Chinese plantings, a trickling waterfall, and a goldfish pool. A tinted glass dome overhead simulates the sky and suggests its traditional use as an open-air moon-viewing terrace in its native setting. Even on the sunniest days, the installation is cast in a diffused, dreamy twilight.

Garden courtyards in China were often given poetic names by their scholar owners. This one, appropriately enough, is called "In Search of Quietude."

Visitor's Note: Two other Met destinations promise ample repose. The **Temple of Dendur** *in the Egyptian wing, with its slanted 40-foot glass wall and black reflection pool, is almost eerily quiet. Seasonally, you can also enjoy the* **Cantor Roof Garden** *on the fifth floor. Part wood deck, part stone terrace, the garden offers memorable treetop views of Central Park.*

Bartow-Pell **Mansion Museum**

Address: 895 Shore Rd., Pelham Bay Park, Bronx
Phone: (718) 885-1461
Hours: Museum open Wednesday, Saturday,
and Sunday, noon to 4 P.M.;
grounds open daily during daylight hours
Admission: $5 for museum tour; free to grounds
Subway: 6 to Pelham Bay stop, then take
bus below
Bus: 45 Westchester-Bee Line to gates
(no bus Sundays)
Auto: Call for directions
Website: www.bpmm.org

a t some time or another, every New Yorker contracts a serious case of "urbanitis"—a nagging disease for which I know only one cure: trees, grass, and open space. On those days when even Central Park lacks adequate healing power, consider a day trip to the lovingly restored Bartow-Pell Mansion in the Bronx, where you will find ample doses of those much-needed antidotes.

Although located near the Westchester border, Bartow-Pell is surprisingly accessible by public transportation. Peering up the winding drive and wooded estate grounds from the mansion's massive entrance gates, I am always filled with a splendid anticipation of the country elegance lying just ahead.

The mansion, one of the finest examples of early Greek Revival architecture in America, is famous for its seashell-shaped, three-story hanging staircase, a gravity-defying marvel of construction. The self-guided tour includes a visit to a pleasant orangery— a French-style greenhouse room—where strong southern light warms the chilliest of winter days.

Outside, explore the mansion's nine-and-a-half rolling acres, including the walled formal gardens with lawns that spill seamlessly into nearby Long Island Sound. The cure for city claustrophobia reaches its full potency after you've walked the property's well-marked paths through unspoiled forests and marshlands, or ventured to the bordering Siwanoy Hiking Trail through more than two thousand acres of surrounding Pelham Bay Park. Got a case of urbanitis? Take a two-hour hike in undisturbed wilderness and call me in the morning.

The Broken Kilometer

Address: 393 West Broadway, bet. Broome
and Spring Sts.
Phone: (212) 989-5566
Hours: Wednesday through Sunday, noon to
6 P.M.; closed July and August
Admission: Free
Subway: N, R to Prince St., walk west
Bus: M1, 6 (Broadway) to Prince St.
Website: www.brokenkilometer.org

It may look like an enormous metal xylophone, but there's no music playing at *The Broken Kilometer*. In fact, it's the silence and stillness permeating the sculpture's huge gallery space that makes a visit here so memorable.

Tucked behind a discreet façade in SoHo, *The Broken Kilometer* consists of five hundred solid brass rods lying side by side in five parallel rows. Each circular rod is more than 6.5 feet (2 meters) long and 2 inches wide, and if laid end to end would measure 1 kilometer. The precise placement of the bars, in a spacious setting 45 feet wide by 125 feet long, is so startling that it takes a couple of minutes to fully register the sight.

Installed here by artist Walter De Maria in 1979, *The Broken Kilometer* still attracts fewer than fifty visitors a day. You'll frequently find yourself alone (a curator sits at a small corner desk), with plenty of privacy to enjoy the sculpture's serene subtleties. A taut nylon rope prevents you from walking among the shiny rods, but you can pass back and forth along its width, which appears to set the bars in motion: One minute *The Broken Kilometer* is a frozen sea of brass, the next it shimmers and dances in wavelike rhythms. A metal halide lighting system creates a daylight effect, further animating the sculpture.

Resist the temptation to move on before *The Broken Kilometer* has shown you its changeability and moods. Stand in the gallery's far left corner and use the sculpture as a meditative visual field. Breathe and repeat.

Cherry Walk at
the Hudson River

Address: 100th St. to 125th St.;
enter Riverside Park at 98th St., walk west
to the river
Phone: 800-201-PARK
Hours: Daily, dawn to dusk
Admission: Free
Subway: 1 to 96th St., walk five minutes west
Bus: M5, M104 to 100th St.

C onsecrated by the feet of a hundred
thousand serenity-seekers: that's how I think of
Cherry Walk, the narrow ribbon of land that
meanders along the Hudson River between
100th and 125th Streets.

The ambling masses have been so devoted to this
simple but seductive footpath for decades that
the Parks Department finally decided to make it
official. Several years ago, the city tastefully and
artistically paved the single track of dirt and
christened it Cherry Walk, in honor of the
pervasive cherry trees that explode with puffed

blossoms and fragrance along both sides of the
Henry Hudson Parkway in the spring.

Sensitive landscape architects have managed to
preserve all the grace this shoulder of grass and
trees has to offer. Not more than 30 feet wide in
most places, the macadam walkway serpentines
between trees and quarried granite boulders,
which have been strategically placed for intermit-
tent rest stops and riverside contemplation.
At the shoreline, massive flat stones slope gently
toward the water and provide an inviting place
to remove your shoes or rollerblades and
lean back to face the sun, while the tidal surge
licks and laps at your feet.

Despite its proximity to the highway,
Cherry Walk seems remarkably insulated from
the traffic—you can easily saunter along, almost
oblivious to the passing cars. People who have
loved this hospitable path since it was just a
rutted trail have always known this. Now you
can make that pleasant discovery, too.

Chopra Center and Spa

Address: 1710 Broadway at 54th St.
Phone: (212) 246-7600
Hours: Monday through Friday, 10 A.M. to 9 P.M.; Saturday and Sunday, 10 A.M. to 7 P.M.
Admission: Free for the Meditation Room; spa services from $45
Subway: N, R to 57th Street, walk west
Bus: M6, 7 (Seventh Ave.) to 54th Street
Website: www.chopracenterny.com

deepak Chopra is everywhere. With more than forty books on alternative medicine, spirituality, emotional healing, and meditation, the Indian medical doctor turned health guru has reshaped the way many Americans think about mind, body, and soul. His blissful healing center and spa in Manhattan is making an equally powerful impression on many New Yorkers, and for good reason.

They have succeeded in creating such a thoroughly pleasing and transformative environment here—one that seems to transport you from Midtown to the finest retreat spas of New Mexico or California in minutes—that I doubt you'll find a better spot for serene detoxification in the city. Based on ayurveda, an ancient Indian discipline considered the "mother science of healing," I have rarely had as sensual, relaxing, and nourishing a treatment as my amara clarifying facial at the Chopra Center. More than just revitalizing to my face, the one-hour experience seemed to nurture all my senses, from the feel of the thick, silky robe I wore, to the sounds of the soothing music they played, and the hypnotic aroma of the essential oils they rubbed into my skin. I was an instant devotee. Best of all, my restored sense of inner peace didn't wash off.

The extraordinary Chopra Center is not all about pricey spa treatments, either. Advancing Chopra's idea that war and violence can be defeated when a critical mass of people focus on peace, the center offers a Sundays for Peace group meditation, as well as daily guided meditation, or use of their mellow meditation room at any time—all free. Check the website for schedules.

The Cloisters

Address: Northern tip of Fort Tryon Park
Phone: (212) 923-3700
Hours: Tuesday through Sunday, 9:30 A.M. to
5:15 P.M.
Admission: $12 suggested donation
Subway: A to 190th St., walk ten minutes north
Bus: M4 directly to the Cloisters
Website: www.metmuseum.org

In medieval Europe, cloisters were central to monastic life. Protected from the outside world, monks were able to walk quietly in contemplation, meditate, read religious texts, and tend flower and medicinal herb gardens. Our own Cloisters in upper Manhattan is such an exquisite reconstruction of a medieval monastery—architecturally and atmospherically—that it has become a cherished urban sanctuary for many New Yorkers. The utter serenity of this hilltop structure is a rare gift that's always appreciated.

The Cloisters opened as a branch of the Metropolitan Museum of Art in 1938 on family property donated by John D. Rockefeller. (To ensure that the arcadian views would be preserved, Rockefeller also purchased a tract of land directly across the river in New Jersey.) He then shipped original architectural elements from five cloisters in France to be reconstructed as the centerpieces of this medieval world high above the Hudson.

Built to house the museum's medieval art collection, everything here is authentic—from the magnificent Unicorn tapestries and Romanesque colonnades to the cobblestoned courtyards and grotesque stone gargoyles. Haunting Gregorian chanting fills the air as you pass through the vaulted passageways.

The three cloister gardens have been rigorously researched to ensure that the hundreds of plant and herb varieties were familiar to monks during the Middle Ages. There is a particularly beautiful espaliered pear tree—now almost seventy years old—that grows in the Bonnefont herb garden. It should not be missed.

Conservatory Garden

Address: 105th St. and Fifth Ave.
Phone: (212) 860-1382
Hours: Daily, 8 A.M. to dusk
Admission: Free
Subway: 6 to 103rd St., walk west
Bus: M1, 2, 3, 4 (Fifth or Madison Aves.) to 105th St.
Website: www.centralparknyc.org

i have begged and pleaded. I have cajoled and coerced. I have heralded the special joys of the Conservatory Garden in every edition of this book. And yet it still remains one of the prettiest, most pristine secrets in Manhattan.

There was a period in the 1960s and '70s when this area was suspect and people stayed away. Those days are long past, and the six-acre site—New York's only formal garden—is now both safe and sensational. Pampered and protected by a full-time staff, this robust, four-season garden is as inviting in February, when the buttery hellebores come out, as it is in May, when tens of thousands of tulips and narcissus make their brilliant appearance.

Whenever I enter the huge wrought-iron gates, I feel as if I've stepped into the sweeping backyard of a stately English home (although there are French and Italian influences here, too). The precisely trimmed hedges, enchanting arbors, romantic crab-apple allées, sculpted fountains, and huge wisteria pergola all contribute to the garden's Victorian ambience.

The south end, also called "the Secret Garden" as a tribute to the Frances Hodgson Burnett children's classic, seems always to be filled with birdsong. It has particular charm, with a whimsical fountain, hidden niches, and bountiful flowerbeds.

*Traveler's Note: Five blocks north through the park, the once-decaying **Harlem Meer** has been transformed from a swampy soup of algae and detritus into pristine wetlands and sandy beach. It's worth the walk.*

Urban D'Mai Spa

Address: 157 Fifth Ave., bet. Lincoln and
St. Johns Places, Brooklyn
Phone: (718) 398-2100
Hours: Monday, Tuesday, Wednesday, Friday,
11 A.M. to 7:30 P.M.;
Thursday, 11 A.M. to 9 P.M.; Saturday and
Sunday, 10 A.M. to 7 P.M.
Admission: Spa services from $65
Subway: R to Union/Fourth Ave., walk east
Website: www.dmaiurbanspa.com

In the past decade, day spas have invaded
New York. This is not a bad thing. With rest and
rejuvenation available on virtually every corner,
our "calm quotient" inevitably goes up. But how
do you know the best places to go to?

Start with D'Mai Urban Spa in Brooklyn, where
the Balinese themes reinforce the feeling that
you've arrived at a faraway escape. The dominant
design feature is a 70-foot interior boardwalk of
white cedar, framed on both sides by a silent
stream of smooth, gray river pebbles. Spanning
the length of the spa and dotted with lounge
chairs, you could rest contentedly by this

planked path in your silk robe and slippers for hours . . . but skilled hands await you.

A good massage can drop tension like a stone, and at D'Mai the stress-neutralizing benefits are multiplied in settings like the Cabana room—a tented, healing haven poised below a shaded skylight. During my deep-tissue massage, rain fell lightly, showering the room's ceiling with a soporific pitter-patter. On the floor, visible below my face cradle, was a bowl of fragrant orchids. Later, I was handed a glass of cool spring water with cucumber slices. Details like these make D'Mai truly special.

For excellent massage in spacious, subdued surroundings, you can also try **Kneaded Bodyworks** (518 Fifth Ave. at 43rd St., 212-642-4307, www.kneadedbodyworks.com), where the staff's determination to make every customer happy impressed me. The superheated sauna experience in the Hwangto igloo at **Athena Spa** (32 East 31st St., 212-683-4484, www.athenaspany31.com) proved to be the perfect complement to my foot reflexology. Feel confident beginning your plan of inaction at any one of these healing destinations.

The Elevated Acre

Address: 55 Water St. at Old Slip Rd.
Phone: (212) 747-9120
Hours: Daily; May 1 through Sept. 30,
7 A.M. to 10 P.M.;
Oct. 1 through April 30, 8 A.M. to 8 P.M.
Admission: Free
Subway: N, R to Whitehall St., walk east
Bus: M15 (First and Second Aves.) to South Ferry
Website: www.elevatedacre.com

a friend living in the Financial District mentioned a dunelike public plaza just a few blocks from her home where she enjoyed journal writing over her morning coffee. Virtually invisible from the street, the Elevated Acre, I realized, was a bona fide, hidden oasis when I passed by twice before locating the access escalator.

This rooftop plaza at 55 Water Street was featureless and uninviting until a $7 million renovation in 2005 transformed the nearly one acre of terrace into a superb parklike setting. Designed with a rising slope that crests onto a wide-plank boardwalk overlooking the

East River, you won't find better views of
New York Harbor or Governor's Island.

Landscaped areas are planted with native species
and beautiful dune grasses that gently swish in the
breeze, the sound masking the drone from FDR
Drive, which passes below the plaza's eastern
border. Teak benches are strategically placed so
that they're shielded by the high grasses, creating
quiet recesses for reading or conversation. Facing
north and west is an elaborate structure of poured
concrete steps offering more outdoor seating as
it tiers down to a 7,000-square-foot grassy area.

The Elevated Acre's most striking feature is a
rectangular beacon with a grid surface of glass,
rising 50 feet above the street. This high-tech,
LED lantern is lit nightly in themed color
combinations (such as red and green for
Christmas, or red and pink for Valentine's Day)
and anchors the relaxed setting.

*Patriot's Note: Follow the plaza's southeast steps to
the **Vietnam Veterans Memorial** nearby. You'll be
moved by the evocative, glass-brick "letter wall."*

Equitable Tower Atrium

**Address: 787 Seventh Ave., bet. 51st and
52nd Sts.**
Hours: Daily, 10 A.M. to 6 P.M.
Admission: Free
Subway: N, R to 49th St.; 1 to 50th St.
Bus: M6, 7 (Seventh Ave.) to 51st St.

Y ou're being jostled and jabbed, spinning

along the sidewalk storm called Midtown

when, right in the eye of the hurricane,

you suddenly notice a dramatic cessation

of sensory assaults.

This gift of solitude is tucked into the 40-foot,

semicircular marble settee in the Equitable

Tower Atrium. The curving bench is a sculptural,

spatial, and acoustical phenomenon. I will never

understand how it works, but take just a few

steps inside this skylit crescent and you have the

distinct sensation of being held firmly in a noise-

muting, marble cocoon. Add the flora-filled

marble fountain and dense screen of tropical

conifers, and it becomes nearly impossible

to leave this protective embrace.

You'll marvel at Roy Lichenstein's *Mural with

Blue Brushstroke*, a monumental piece that

dominates the wall behind the bench enclosure,

painted onsite by the Pop artist in 1984.

But, personally, I ask little more of this spotless

atrium space than to rest my city weariness

upon its cool surfaces.

Traveler's Note: Generous financial incentives to

developers who provide public atriums and open

spaces have resulted in a contrasting mix of

macabre, mall-like settings and truly splendid

escapes. Here are some others that I rate highly:

*the **Continental Atrium**'s (Maiden Lane and*

Front St.) intricate Tinkertoy-like interior is a

*playful place to relax; the **Deutsche Bank***

***Building** (60 Wall St.) adds rotating art dis-*

*plays to the ample seating; and the former **IBM***

***Building** (590 Madison Ave. at 56th St.) is still a*

fine oasis, with its skylit bamboo court and con-

servatory.

Erol Beker Chapel
in St. Peter's Church

Address: Lexington Ave. at 54th St.
Phone: (212) 935-2200
Hours: Daily, 8 A.M. to 8 P.M.
Admission: Free
Subway: 6 to 51st St.
Bus: M101, 102 (Lexington and Third Aves.) to 51st St.
Website: www.saintpeters.org

If you could design a "place of purity" in New York City, what would it look like and where would it be? Louise Nevelson, the acclaimed American sculptor, was given exactly this task in the mid-seventies, and she proceeded to transform a sliver of Midtown land into a private corner of celestial calm, a hushed and happy place called the Erol Beker Chapel.

As much an exuberant work of modern art as a dulcet haven for heart and soul, the chapel is Nevelson's only permanent sculptural environment in New York. She wanted this unique prayer and meditation space, tucked inside the north wall of St. Peter's Church (the jagged appendage at the base of the Citicorp complex), to exude purity. That's why almost everything in this 28-by-21-foot, five-sided chapel is white: white painted sculptural elements on white walls, white columns, a white sanctuary lamp, and white frosted windows. Even the floors, altar, and pews (with off-white cushions) are made of a light bleached ash.

Nevelson's *The Cross of the Good Shepherd*—a heavily stylized sculpture loosely suggestive of a traditional crucifix—sits against a field of gold leaf on the north wall, giving the eye a calming focal point from which the surroundings gently fall away. I am unable to pass within five blocks of this little pocket of peace without its enthralling gravity drawing me in. The stillness here is palpable. Just gaze into the solitary sanctuary lamp for a minute, and you'll return to the streets a more agreeable human being.

Ford Foundation Building

**Address: 320 East 43rd St., bet. First and
Second Aves.**
Phone: (212) 573-5000
**Hours: Monday through Friday, 10 A.M. to
4 P.M.**
Admission: Free
**Subway: 4, 5, 6 to Grand Central, walk east
Bus: M15 (First and Second Aves.) to 42nd St.;
M104 or M42 (crosstown) to Second Ave.**

In a stroke of architectural genius, the designer of the Ford Foundation, Kevin Roche, placed the building around the park, instead of the other way around. Here you can enjoy a 160-foot-high, glass-walled, one-third-acre terraced garden, lushly landscaped with exotic greenery.

Because there are no formal benches or chairs, and no food or drink allowed, Roche's towering greenhouse plaza does not draw the kind of crowds that other public spaces seem to attract. In fact, the rain-forestlike atrium is frequently unoccupied.

You'll be most comfortable ascending to the east side of the top tier, where a low sun-drenched sitting wall provides a quiet vantage point from which to study the 17 full-grown trees (including acacia, Norfolk pine, and eucalyptus), 1,000 shrubs, 150 vines, and nearly 22,000 ground-cover plants. The landscapers also rotate seasonal plantings, with tulips in spring, begonias in summer, chrysanthemums in fall, and poinsettias in winter. The three levels of garden court are lined with brick pathways descending to a still-water pool, into which you can drop your coins to benefit UNICEF. Rainwater is captured in cisterns on the roof to feed this pool and irrigate the garden during water shortages.

At the Ford Foundation, the air is dense with the earthy scent of bursting horticulture, a kind of intoxicating chlorophyll panacea guaranteed to calm the most hyperactive minds.

Gantry Plaza State Park

Address: 474 48th Ave., Queens
Phone: (718) 786-6385
Hours: Daily, dawn to 1 A.M.
Admission: Free
Subway: 7, one stop from Grand Central to
Vernon-Jackson Ave., Queens; walk west on
48th Ave. to the river
Bus: B61 and Q103 to Vernon Blvd./Jackson Ave.

more pier than park, Gantry Plaza is a jewel on the Queens waterfront. The four parallel piers, each with its own signature identity and distinct features, have turned a former blot along the East River into one of the city's finest examples of urban restoration.

Built to encompass two huge gantries—waterfront cranes used to load and unload floating rail cars during this area's industrial heyday—the two-and-a-half acre park has won awards for its striking design and sensitive use of the natural shoreline. And it will get better. Future phases of the development plan call for nineteen acres of stress-relieving park, serving shoreline lovers, bird-watchers, ballplayers, picnickers, sunbathers, strollers, evening romantics, and moon gazers.

Just one stop on the 7 train from Grand Central Station, Gantry Plaza State Park is quick to reach from Manhattan and worth the trip. At the center of the park complex are the looming black gantries emblazoned with the words "Long Island" in faded red letters. Fishing is permitted on the southernmost pier, where you'll find a wavelike 40-foot bench and a large stainless-steel table for cleaning your catch. I prefer the second pier, with its four wooden chaise longues fixed in place to face the southern sun.

Farther north, you'll find dozens of big boulders shaved flat so that you can sit on top, as well as high-backed throne chairs dotting the water's edge. They're located near the famous neon Pepsi-Cola sign that you see in Long Island City when looking east from Midtown.

Now imagine the views looking back.

The General
Theological
Seminary

**Address: 175 Ninth Ave., bet. 20th and
21st Sts.
Phone: (212) 243-5150
Hours: March through October, Monday
through Saturday, 9 A.M. to
5 P.M.; November through February,
9 A.M. to 3 P.M.; closed Sunday
Admission: Free
Subway: A, C, E to 23rd St.; 1 to 18th St.
Bus: M11 (Ninth and Tenth Aves.) to 23rd St.
Website: www.gts.edu**

Once an apple orchard donated to the Episcopal Church by Clement Clarke Moore (author of "A Visit from St. Nicholas"), the shaded grounds of this seminary have been a heavenly urban getaway since the mid-1800s. Here you'll find the pastoral serenity of a New England campus quad seamlessly meshed with the cloistered formality of a collegiate English close.

The first time I entered the pristine setting (you must sign in at the Ninth Avenue entrance), I was utterly amazed that this space was open to the public. It really is that idyllic. But the seminarians here are extraordinarily friendly people who want to contribute to their community, and have done so with this generous outdoor "peace offering."

The red brick buildings that frame the seminary grounds were built beginning in 1836 and cover an entire city block. While in some disrepair, they are nevertheless exquisite examples of nineteenth-century Gothic Revival architecture and one of the reasons this complex is registered as a National Historic Landmark.

Don't miss the Chapel of the Good Shepherd at the heart of the block-long quad. It's a charming, simple, countrylike chapel that glows with the warmth of beautiful stained glass and dark, rich woodcarvings. After strolling the landscaped pathways of the seminary's outer yard—dotted with mature and majestic oak, birch, elm, and linden trees—I've always found the chapel an ideal place to explore my own inner pathways.

Greenacre Park

**Address: 221 East 51st St., bet. Second
and Third Aves.
Hours: Daily, 8 A.M. to 6 P.M.;
in summer, until 8 P.M.
Admission: Free
Subway: E or F to 53rd St.; 6 to 51st St.,
walk east
Bus: M101 (Lexington and Third Aves.)
to 51st St.**

the brilliant landscape architect Hideo Sasaki
created this vest-pocket park in the early 1970s.
According to him, the primary design goal was
"to provide a place for the general public to gain
special repose from the increasing city
experience of noise, concrete, and humdrum."
New Yorkers have been grateful for
his vision ever since.

This diminutive park in the heart of the east
Midtown commercial and residential district is
nowhere near an acre in size (it's just 110 feet
deep by 60 feet wide), but perhaps because green

space is such a rarity in this neighborhood, it seems to offer an acre's worth of tranquility. Like Paley Park, its smaller cousin a few blocks away on East 53rd Street, Greenacre Park boasts a dramatic two-story waterfall, this one constructed of massive granite blocks. There's a babbling brook here, too, that ambles along the east wall and empties into a plunge pool. The intermingling sounds of gurgling, flowing, and cascading water significantly mask the street noise, insulating this pleasant park from the incessant throb of the city.

I particularly recommend the park on rainy days, when you can ponder the waterfalls alone, undisturbed, and comfortably dry under the trellis roof of the west terrace. While always a fine urban escape, be advised that, in good weather, Greenacre Park is a magnet for local office workers, who swarm here to soak in the sun and relative quiet during lunch hour.

Green-Wood Cemetery

Address: Fifth Ave. at 25th St., Brooklyn
Phone: (718) 768-7300
Hours: Daily, 8 A.M. to 4 P.M.
Admission: Free
Subway: N, R to 25th St., walk east
Auto: Brooklyn-Battery Tunnel to the Brooklyn-
Queens Expressway (BQE), to Third Ave. exit,
left on 25th St. to Fifth Ave.
Website: www.greenwoodcemetery.org

forget for a moment that there are five hundred thousand dead people here.

Consider instead that this urban cemetery was designed in 1838 by civil engineer David Bates Douglass as a pastoral park, with rolling hills, five lakes, 30 miles of serpentine pathways, and some of the city's oldest trees—all in a bucolic setting half the size of Central Park.

Within this sepulchral masterpiece situated at the highest point in Brooklyn, you'll find no cars, no trucks, no subways, no sirens, no screaming kids, and virtually no (living) people. The stillness here is profound, much like you'd find at, well, a cemetery.

Green-Wood has the additional appeal of its celebrity occupants, among whom are stained-glass master Louis Comfort Tiffany, pencil man Eberhard Faber, piano maker Henry Steinway, sewing-machine inventor Elias Howe (along with his dog, Fannie), soap magnate William Colgate, and composer Leonard Bernstein. As for why Green-Wood Cemetery has a particularly magical air, perhaps it's because this is also the eternal resting place of actor Frank Morgan. You know . . . *The Wizard of Oz.*

Traveler's Note: Designated a National Historic Landmark in the fall of 2006, Green-Wood encourages public visitation and is also a favorite destination for bird-watchers. Guided tours of the famous monuments are conducted year-round. Call ahead or check the website for schedules and gathering locations.

Inwood Hill Park

Address: 207th St. and Seaman Ave.
Hours: Daily, dawn to dusk
Admission: Free
Subway: A, 1 to 207th St.
Bus: M100 (Amsterdam Ave.) to 207th St.

my childhood home bordered a large, wooded nature preserve. From my bedroom window, I viewed this seemingly endless forest as a dark, dangerous place. But as I grew older, it became a friend—a private world to wander in, to ponder my future without disturbance, to conjure grand visions, or even to cry when necessary, openly and unobserved.

I have been able to reconnect with that secret forest of my childhood at Inwood Hill Park. This beautiful, rustic, rocky park is the largest expanse of natural woodland left in Manhattan. You can walk along miles of meandering pathways within its 196-acre wilderness, or blaze your own trails over mossy glens, fallen trees, and sparse under-brush. Flag down one of the patrolling Urban Park Rangers to secure a trail map.

Inwood Park holds two special surprises: the mysterious Indian Caves that remain largely undisturbed (located at the park's center, near Pothole Road on the map), and Manhattan's only remaining salt marsh, in the valley section of the park. Visit this brackish habitat to spy herons, egrets, hawks, and an occasional raccoon bobbing for oysters.

Historians will note the marked boulder where it is believed Peter Minuit bought Manhattan Island from the Reckgawawanc Indians for trinkets worth about 60 Dutch guilders. Proves what I often say— you just can't stretch a guilder the way you used to.

Traveler's Note: Look for the cliff outcroppings overlooking the Hudson River at the western edge of the park. You can sometimes shimmy through a rolled-back fence opening to the most scenic picnicking spot in the city.

Isamu Noguchi
Garden Museum

Address: 9-01 33rd Rd., bet. Vernon Blvd. and
10th St., Queens
Phone: (718) 204-7088
Hours: Wednesday, Thursday, Friday, 10 A.M. to
5 P.M.; Saturday and Sunday, 11 A.M. to
6 P.M.; closed Monday and Tuesday
Admission: $10
Subway: N to Broadway (Long Island City),
walk west ten blocks to Vernon Blvd.,
south two blocks to the museum
Sunday shuttle bus: Call for information
Website: www.noguchi.org

Isamu Noguchi, the late Japanese–American sculptor, would sometimes study a piece of raw marble or granite for years before making his first strike. He called this process "discovering the stone's essence."

At the Isamu Noguchi Garden Museum, you can almost feel the master artist urging you to take up your own, inner sculpting tools—to patiently split, cut, chisel, and polish your way to discovering the essence of self. Noguchi's sculptures always speak this personally and deeply.

This dignified, uncluttered gallery and garden is situated in the otherwise bustling heart of Long Island City's industrial waterfront—a site Noguchi chose for its proximity to the marble-cutting shops that were once in the area. The museum, part raw cinderblock open to the elements, part former industrial plant, contains more than 250 Noguchi sculptures of stone, metal, wood, and clay. Each is placed with precision and sensitivity to elicit the most profound reaction. The peacefulness of the sculpture garden alone, enjoyed year round by a family of mourning doves, rewards your extra effort in getting here. A half-day trip is advisable, so you'll have time to absorb the illuminating messages Noguchi has chiseled into his oracular boulders.

Traveler's Note: From the museum, walk two blocks north to **Socrates Sculpture Park***, a rugged, unruly, riverfront creation that's home to outdoor sculpture on a towering scale, and very peaceful. You'll see.*

The Jacqueline Onassis Reservoir Running Path

Address: Central Park; enter at 90th St.
and Fifth Ave.
Hours: Daily, 24 hours
Admission: Free
Subway: 4, 5, 6 to 86th St., walk west to
entrance
Bus: M1, 2, 3, 4 to 86th St.

Y ou've certainly heard of the "runner's high," that state of quasi-euphoria that every serious aerobic athlete experiences. In New York, we have a unique version called the "reservoir runner's high." It kicks in with sweet reliability after a lap or two around the historic reservoir path, perhaps the most famous jogging track in the country.

This big (by Manhattan standards) body of water attracts a large variety of migrating waterfowl, along with the normal contingent of native mallards, loons, and seagulls. A bridle path runs parallel to the track for much of its length, so it's not unusual to find yourself matching strides with an equestrian or two. The combined effect makes a circuit of the elevated, 1.6-mile cinder path the equivalent of jogging the perimeter of a country lake.

You'll pass other runners along the way (path etiquette calls for counter clockwise revolutions), but these are conscientious, quiet athletes. It's a civilized group. And if you stand by the South Gate House (86th Street, looking due north), you'll see one of my favorite sights in Manhattan—a buildingless horizon. You can cast your gaze far out into the distance from here and behold only water, trees, and flocks of birds. What a relief for skyscraped eyes.

The congenial reservoir path is more than a spot for furtive celebrity watching (the loop attracts many recognizable runners); it's a refreshing island of water in a big stone sea. Drink deeply.

Jacques Marchais
Museum of Tibetan Art

Address: 338 Lighthouse Ave., Staten Island
Phone: (718) 987-3500
Hours: February through December,
Wednesday through Sunday, 1 P.M. to
5 P.M.; in January, by appointment only
Admission: $5 adults; children free
Bus: From the Staten Island Ferry, take S74 to
Lighthouse Ave., then walk ten minutes uphill
(allow ninety minutes total travel
from Manhattan)
Auto: Call for directions
Website: www.tibetanmuseum.com

This cliff-clinging museum on Staten Island incorporates a replica of a Tibetan mountain temple that is so authentic, Buddhist monks come here to perform rituals and religious practices.

The creation of Jacqueline Klauber, an American woman who was an avid collector of Tibetan and Himalayan art (she used the name Jacques Marchais for professional purposes), the monastery museum holds one of the largest collections of Tibetan art outside of Tibet. The lamasery altar is so jam-packed with gilded

Buddhas, ornate prayer wheels, and elaborate incense burners, you'll wonder how peaceful prayer ever happens here . . . until you let the transformative powers of these sacred objects envelop you.

While there are no Himalayan vistas, the museum is located at the highest point on the Eastern Seaboard, and the distant harbor views are a favorite local secret. On the tranquil patio garden, you'll also find huge baboons, trumpeting elephants, and prancing rabbits . . . all of the stone variety. The goldfish in the lotus pond, however, are real.

Look beyond the graceful altar and marble Buddha to the colorful prayer flags fluttering in the trees. It is believed that the wind carries their blessings and messages out to the world. I prayed for more places like this one.

Traveler's Note: The museum has an extensive calendar of Far East–related events. Call or visit the website for listings.

Jamaica Bay
Wildlife Refuge

**Address: Cross Bay Blvd., Broad Channel,
Queens**
Phone: (718) 318-4340
**Hours: Trails open daily, sunrise to sunset;
visitors' center open from 8:30 A.M. to 5 P.M.**
Admission: Free
**Subway: A to Broad Channel, walk west to
Cross Bay Blvd., turn right (north), walk half a
mile to the visitors' center**
Auto: Call for directions

this place is for the birds—piping plovers, blue herons, snowy egrets, Canada geese, warblers, ospreys, barn owls, and about three hundred other species that have been spotted throughout the 9,100 acres of this diverse habitat.

The Jamaica Bay Wildlife Refuge is located on the Atlantic Flyway—an important seasonal migration route—and provides a layover point for birds resting and feeding in the sanctuary's salt marshes, freshwater ponds, woods, and wetlands. Known nationally among birders as a hotspot, the wide cinder trails are clustered with bird watchers toting cameras and binoculars, silently observing their subjects nesting, resting, fishing, and preening.

After you've stopped at the visitors' center, make your way around the 1.5-mile West Pond trail. Despite its close proximity to Kennedy Airport, the refuge is located far enough from the flight paths of those soaring metal birds to ensure water-washed solitude for your nature stroll. While easily walked in an hour, the restorative benefits of this shore-hugging trail increase if you take your time. Stop at every strategically placed viewing bench, turn at every side trail (like the terrapin nesting path that leads to a beach at the tip of the peninsula), and read every guide marker with information on native flora and fauna.

A friend and I wandered slowly through the secluded upland trails, where we startled a quail in the scrub (and it startled us), spotted a cardinal perched on a pine bough, and watched ring-necked ducks waddle through the reeds—a fully gratifying wildlife experience with the Manhattan skyline visible in the distance.

John Finley Walk at Carl Schurz Park

Address: Enter at 86th St. and East End Ave.
Hours: Daily, dawn to 1 A.M.
Admission: Free
Subway: 4, 5, 6 to 86th St.
Bus: M86 (86th St. crosstown) to York Ave.,
walk east; M31 (York Ave.) to 86th St.

the broad, sweeping, two-sided staircase that rises up to John Finley Walk from 86th Street portends something special lying just beyond. As you make your way to the top of those significant stone steps, the mystery reveals itself in exhilarating views of the East River from every point along this historic promenade.

John Finley Walk is encompassed by Carl Schurz Park—one of those places in the city you know you've heard of, but can't quite pinpoint. Or so it seems, given that this reliable, four-season refuge is often lightly populated. The smallish, ten-acre neighborhood park and its century-old esplanade run along the eastern property line of Gracie Mansion (Hizzoner's house) making it a safe place to amble at any time of the day or night.

Carl Schurz serves respite-seekers of all ages, from young families to elderly local residents. Leisurely strollers walk in small clusters chatting amiably, gazing out at the remarkable riverscape and Roosevelt Island. The casual pace is infectious. And the views are particularly breath-taking at night when the river bridges are lit, throwing luminous reflections off the water.

There's a children's playground at the south end that can be boisterous, so for optimum privacy walk north along the promenade past the flagpole to where the footpath narrows and bends to the right. Continue for another 100 feet (if you reach the fireboat house, you've gone too far) and settle yourself down on a shaded bench against the hillside. You'll know when you've reached the right place by that telltale sound— the sound of silence.

Kayaking on the Hudson River

Address: Three locations—Pier 40 at Houston
St.; Pier 96 at 56th St.;
and 72nd St. along the river walkway
Phone: (646) 613-0740
Hours: Mid-May through mid-October;
Saturdays, Sundays, and holidays, 9 A.M. to
6 P.M.; weekday evenings at 56th St., 5 P.M. to
7 P.M.
Admission: Free
Subway/Bus: Check website
Website: www.downtownboathouse.org

For avid kayakers, the Hudson River is considered "Big Water"—powerful, demanding, deserving of respect. Despite the tricky currents, strong winds, and floating detritus, it is possible to experience this tidal river safely, with profound intimacy, in a kayak.

By law, the city has to provide public access to navigable waters from designated piers and boat launches. In this case, they've authorized the volunteer, not-for-profit Downtown Boathouse to offer education and easy access for canoeists and kayakers. And, incredibly, it's all free—use of the kayaks, basic instruction, and your time spent on the water.

Under the responsible, safety-first tutelage of these dedicated volunteers, you're given a life vest, oar, and kayak, and sent off to paddle the relatively protected waters of the adjacent embayments. The public kayaks, virtually roll-proof and excellent for beginners, are called "sit-on-tops" because they have no cockpit.

Once you're bobbing on the water—just body, boat, and blade—you experience what veteran "river rats" describe as a transcendent union with your surroundings: expansive water, open sky, the light slapping of water ripples against the boat, the swish of your oar. You see the busyness and the bustle on shore, but you are not there. You are not in the city at all. You are here, immersed in liquid nature.

*River Rats' Note: If kayaking captures your attention (and it easily can), contact the **New York Kayak Company** (1-800-KAYAK99/ www.nykayak.com) for expert instruction and all-day sea-kayaking adventures.*

La Casa Day Spa Floatation

Address: 41 East 20th St., bet. Park Ave. and
Broadway
Phone: (212) 673-2272
Hours: Float hours are Wednesday, Thursday,
Friday, noon to 8 P.M.; Saturday, 10 A.M. to
6 P.M. Call for appointment.
Admission: $80 for one-hour float/$50 if
combined with any other one-hour treatment
Subway: 4, 5, 6 to 23rd St.
Bus: M101 (Park and Third Aves.) to 20th St.
Website: www.lacasaspa.com

Water is good. Soaking in water so infused
with Epsom salts that you can float weightlessly
in a private sea, tension draining effortlessly
from your body . . . that's really good.

At this health- and detox-oriented day spa,
you will find a state-of-the-art floatation room
with adjoining private shower. All you bring is
your overtaxed body.

As soon as you climb into 8 inches of water so
thoroughly infused with salts that anything (and

anyone) will float, your tightly wound muscles will become completely relaxed, and the warm, silky liquid will rock you into a state of suspended tranquility. By adjusting the light and music levels, you control the degree of sensory input; the fewer external stimuli, the better. Within seconds, your buoyant body surrenders to the anti-gravity effects, and the mind voyage begins.

Some habitual "floaters" claim to experience a level of bliss that takes them back to the threshold of their current incarnation, in the womb. Many first-time floaters have used this liquid cocoon to reach states of profound relaxation and genuine euphoria. Some studies suggest that a two-hour float can be more restful than a full night's sleep. In my case, a lower back spasm I brought into the tank with me had disappeared by the time I dried off.

Yes, water can heal. And the warm waters here, they heal so good.

Lady Mendl's Tea Salon

Address: 56 Irving Pl. at 17th St.
Phone: (212) 533-4466
Hours: Wednesday through Friday, 3 P.M. and
5 P.M. seatings; Saturday and Sunday, 2 P.M.
and 4:30 P.M. seatings
Admission: $35 per person,
reservations required
Subway: 4, 5, 6 to 14th St., walk east
Bus: M1, 2, 3, 4 (Fifth Ave.), walk east
Website: www.ladymendls.com

If everyone in New York were required to break for afternoon tea, I'm sure we'd all feel a bit more civilized and a little less harried.

I've sampled teatime at various places around town in search of the serenity and sophistication associated with this rite, and I think it's done with unusual charm and elegance in the nostalgic parlor of Lady Mendl's Tea Salon. Situated in a lovingly restored 1834 town house in Gramercy Park, the salon is tastefully decorated with upholstered armchairs and antiques of the era, including period china and silver tea services. During winter months, the mellow mood is heightened by the flickering flames from a pair of cozy fireplaces.

The delectable, five-course afternoon tea includes fresh fruit, finger sandwiches, sweet scones with jam, macaroons, and a final sublime pastry offering. More than twenty fine aromatic teas are available, but you will do well to choose the smoky Formosa Oolong or Fancy Ceylon. After an hour and a half of tea and easy conversation at Lady Mendl's, a guest and I concluded our genteel visit to the last century with a stroll around the historic Gramercy Park neighborhood.

While several Midtown hotels also serve afternoon tea, I like the more relaxed ambience at two other downtown cafés: the British flavor of **Tea and Sympathy** (108 Greenwich Ave., 212-989-9735), and **T Salon & T Emporium** (406 Broome St., 212-358-0506) where they aim to change the pace of the world one sip at a time.

Lighthouse Park on Roosevelt Island

Address: Northern tip of Roosevelt Island
Phone: (212) 832-4543
Hours: Daily, 24 hours
Admission: Free
Subway: B, Q to Roosevelt Island
Tram: Departs from 59th St. and Second Ave.
Website: www.rooseveltisland.us

there's nothing like escaping to a quiet island
when the city encroaches on your sanity.
Especially one that is only a five-minute trip
from Midtown Manhattan.

I wonder why so few New Yorkers think of
Roosevelt Island as a viable getaway. Do they
worry they'll get over there and not be able to get
back? Or that the aerial tram will deposit them
in the river before it lands them safely on the
opposite shore? Let me dispel your fears: not
only can you get to tranquil Lighthouse Park

quickly and safely (if you have tram terrors, there's now a subway stop), you can also grab a sandwich, catch a lunchtime half-hour of unobstructed rays, and be back at the office before anyone notices you're gone.

The four-minute tram ride ($1.50 each way) is an event in itself. You can see virtually every inch of Manhattan (most of Queens, too) from 250 feet up on the soaring Swiss cable cars. Once on this sliver of land, take the red minibus (a noteworthy bargain at 25 cents) as far north as it travels, then stroll along the island's west side until you reach the park. You'll probably see a few fishermen near the tiny granite lighthouse and not much else. You'll also find a wide lawn, inviting picnic tables, and a beautiful brick-paved promenade for aimless meandering.

For loafers like me, the extent of island activity involves reclining on a grassy ridge counting barges as they glide by.

Loeb Boathouse
in Central Park

Address: Enter at 72nd St. and Fifth Ave.;
walk 200 yards north
Phone: (212) 517-2233
Hours: March through October, daily, 10 A.M.
to 5 P.M., weather permitting
Admission: $12 per hour per boat
(seats up to five)
Subway: 6 to 68th St., walk west
Bus: M1, 2, 3, 4 (Fifth and Madison Aves.)
to 72nd St.
Website: www.centralpark.com/pages/
attractions/loeb-boathouse.html

this is one place where I guarantee you won't

be bugged or bothered, badgered or bullied.

Even on summer weekends, when many

New Yorkers have the same idea, rowing on

the Central Park Lake is still a wonderful

solitary escape.

After you rent your boat at the Loeb Boathouse,

courteous attendants will assist you with the oars

and requisite life jacket, and then help you cast

off. Wherever you can row, you can go, and with

more than eighteen acres of open water and side pools, you can go far. Pass under the quaint wooden footbridge, watch flocks of waterbirds take flight, skim from a reed bed to a shallow inlet, and take in the surrounding cityscape from your tranquil, mid-lake vantage point.

An ongoing restoration project promises to reclaim silted coves that are currently filled with sediment and overgrown with invasive plants, making them too shallow to navigate. This effort to deepen the lake's waters will also draw more native and migratory birds to Central Park's largest body of water. Bird-watchers have documented sightings of more than 750 different species near the lake, including long-eared owls, snow geese, and red-headed woodpeckers. Whether you're a birder or a boater, this is an idyllic setting for recalibrating your sanity.

Romantics' Note: Inquire at the Loeb Boathouse about spring and summer gondola rides on the lake ($30 for a half-hour).

The Lotus Garden

Address: 97th St. bet. Broadway and
West End Ave.
Hours: April to mid-November, Sunday, 1 P.M.
to 4 P.M. for the public; accessible
at any time for key holders
Admission: Free on Sundays; keys are
$20 for two years
Subway: 1 to 96th St.
Bus: M104 to 96th St.
Website: thelotusgarden.org

there are few things more astonishing in this
city than to witness nature assert itself in
unlikely places—a dandelion rising from a
mound of silt on a rooftop, an oak sapling
poking out from a crack in the sidewalk.

The clearest evidence of nature's reassuring

determination can be found at the remarkable

little Lotus Garden, sitting 20 feet above

97th Street atop a busy parking garage.

Working with local developers in 1983, activists

Mark Greenwald, an architect, and Carrie Maher,

a horticulturist, spearheaded the garden's design with other neighbors. Creating this riot of fragrant color over a garage rooftop involved spreading 3.5 feet of topsoil over the entire 7,000-square-foot expanse.

There are no actual lotus plants in the garden, but you'll find abundant water lilies thriving in two small goldfish ponds. The garden is artfully subdivided into member-tended, productive plots from which grow peach, apple, and cherry trees, fragrant herbs, and bountiful blooms for all seasons.

Though open to the public only on Sundays, you can purchase a key granting you unrestricted two-year access to this elevated oasis for only $20. During a recent visit to this happy shade garden, I strolled the wood chip–lined pathways, wrote in my journal, sniffed the blossoms in a dozen flower beds, then sat pleasantly alone, listening to a choir of chirping sparrows celebrate the day. If there's a better place for which to hold a key, tell me.

The New York Botanical Garden

Address: 200th St. at Southern Blvd., Bronx
Phone: (718) 817-8700
Hours: Tuesday through Sunday, 10 A.M. to
6 P.M.; 5 P.M. in winter
Admission: $6 for grounds only; $13 for
all attractions; on-site parking $5
Train: Metro-North (Harlem Line) from
Grand Central to Botanical Garden stop
Auto: Check website for directions
Website: www.nybg.org

Smell is the most acute of the five senses, a fact that makes a day trip to the New York Botanical Garden one of the most sensual experiences in the city.

Opened in 1902, our nation's largest and oldest botanical garden has 250 paradisiacal acres of blooming, burgeoning, bursting gardens. Add to that the spectacular turn-of-the-century Haupt Conservatory and you have an all-season olfactory feast. The clever horticulturists here have carefully planned a succession of flowers and foliage that keep the grounds in almost full color and fragrance from spring's first thaw to the onset of winter. With so many different habitats here— woodland, rock garden, glade, pond, cultivated rose garden—the staff can be adventurous with its plantings. And the scents engulf you: sweet and spicy, pungent and bitter. The air, laden with nature's infinite perfumes, is a pleasure to breathe.

Let your nose lead you to the heady, organic smells of the last uncut forest in the city, forty acres of hemlock, oak, maple, and hickory (some trees more than 250 years old) crisscrossed with mulch-covered trails. Follow the woodland path to the old fieldstone Snuff Mill—a good place to stop and rest while looking out over the river. There's also a serene conifer forest; the giant evergreens tower above an aromatic bed of balsamic pine needles—perhaps life's most wistful essence.

There are so many pleasurable scents emanating from the Botanical Garden; be prepared to arrive early and leave late. That's the best way to fully inhale New York's most ambrosial experience.

The
New York
Earth Room

Address: 141 Wooster St. (half-block south of
Houston St.)
Phone: (212) 473-8072
Hours: Wednesday through Sunday, noon to
6 P.M. (closed from 3 P.M. to 3:30 P.M.);
closed July and August
Admission: Free
Subway: N, R to Prince St., walk west
Bus: M1, 6 (Broadway) to Prince St.
Website: www.earthroom.org

here's a dirty little secret: One of New York's
most pristine yet peculiar sanctuaries is a SoHo
loft filled with 280,000 pounds of topsoil.

The Earth Room is the creation of artist
Walter De Maria, a man of few words who makes
no attempt to explain his humble earth sculpture.
Nevertheless, this inert, silent scene makes
its own powerful statement about city life—or
more correctly, about the absence of pastoral
simplicity in our lives.

After exclamations of disbelief, you'll be drawn into the disarming vibrations of this austere space, "empty" except for 3,600 square feet of wall-to-wall soil and a few mushrooms. Hunker down behind the low Plexiglas partition so that the huge expanse of earth is at eye level. Breathe in the sweet smell and cool moisture-laden air emanating from the rich black loam. Plunge your hands into the soil—it's allowed. Let the good earth remind you that it always lies softly underfoot, a healing cushion easily forgotten in a city where an impenetrable concrete crust separates you from nature's own terra firma.

Apart from a few regulars who revive themselves weekly at this fragrant, fallow field (along with one overseas businessman who makes a pilgrimage here on every trip, declaring "it's the quietest place in town"), you can call the Earth Room your own. Just don't complain to me when you realize that the dirt has a better apartment than you do.

New York Public Library and Bryant Park

Address: 40th St.–42nd St., bet. Fifth and Sixth Aves.
Phone: (212) 930-0830
Hours: Museum open Monday, Thursday, Friday, Saturday, 10 A.M. to 6 P.M.; Tuesday and Wednesday, 11 A.M. to 7:30 P.M.; Sunday, 1 P.M. to 5 P.M.; park open daily, 8 A.M. to dusk
Admission: Free
Subway: 4, 5, 6 to Grand Central, walk west
Bus: M1, 2, 3, 4 (Fifth and Madison Aves.) to 42nd St.
Website: www.nypl.org

new York's great philanthropists must have anticipated the growing city's need for places of peace and quiet when they financed construction of this massive marble library in 1911. They put more than 630 seats in the Rose Main Reading Room, which would eventually accommodate the hundreds of people who now come here seeking research and refuge. Knowing these visitors would come to expand their minds and imaginations, they painted a muse-worthy ceiling mural of ethereal pink clouds. And to ensure that the library would be a place for rest and renewal, they added a lush green carpet of grass in the back.

This is such a magnificent library, I'm left a little breathless with every visit. The imposing Beaux Arts detailing and architectural grandeur are a reminder of how much books were revered by Americans at the turn of the twentieth century—a respect that is still evident in the vast Rose Room (room 315), which is relatively noise-free despite high usage. If you can finagle a pass to one of the private study rooms, you'll find even more seclusion.

Once sufficiently edified, go out back to the 9.6-acre makeover masterpiece, **Bryant Park**. The park was transformed in the early nineties from a spooky tangle of hedges infested with drug dealers to a secure, superbly conceived city park. The thick-growing lawn, lovingly main-tained perennial borders, and spindly metal café chairs facilitate hours of mindless relaxation. There's free wireless internet access in the park, too, for bouts of online solitaire in the shade.

Nicholas Roerich
Museum

Address: 319 West 107th St., bet. Broadway
and Riverside Dr.
Phone: (212) 864-7752
Hours: Tuesday through Sunday, 2 P.M. to
5 P.M.; closed Mondays
Admission: Free (donations encouraged)
Subway: 1 to 110th St., walk south
Bus: M5, M104 to 107th St.
Website: www.roerich.org

f or many spiritual seekers in the West, the

search for meaning points East—to India,

China, or the Buddhist temples of Tibet.

Some romanticize a trek through the Himalayan

foothills as the ultimate spiritual journey—as

close to God and heaven as you can get with

your feet still on the ground. But if neither your

schedule nor your budget permits a Himalayan

expedition, consider taking a vicarious trek at

the Nicholas Roerich Museum.

This little-known treasury contains more than

two hundred paintings by the Russian-born

Roerich (1874–1947), a mystic, artist, and author who lived in the Himalayas for much of his life. Respected internationally for his efforts to promote peace through culture, Roerich was nominated for the Nobel Peace Prize in 1929. The entire town house is dedicated to his work and spirit, and its casual parlor-style ambience encourages leisurely, deliberate viewing of his expansive mountain scenes.

Allow Roerich's luminous landscape paintings—vibrant with tempera blues, whites, violets, and reds—to lift you up and carry you on a cloud of color to the roof of the world (you can preview these dramatic canvases on the museum's website, but don't let this be a substitute for an actual visit).

There is not a disappointing painting on the entire three floors of this blissful brownstone, but if you really want your soul to fly, go directly to *Kanchenjunga* (front room, second floor). This magnificent image of snow-covered Himalayan peaks will transport you to another realm.

OM Yoga
Center

Address: 826 Broadway, at 12th St.
Phone: (212) 254-9642
Hours: Classes daily from 7 A.M. to 8 P.M.
Admission: Classes start at $12
Subway: 4, 5, 6, N, R to Union Square
Bus: M1, 6 (Broadway) to Union Square
Website: www.omyoga.com

When you practice yoga, you spend a lot of time on your back. That simple observation is what motivated Cyndi Lee, the clever and creative founder of OM Yoga, to paint the ceilings in a soothing palette of earthy colors (the walls remained white) when she opened her spacious yoga center on lower Broadway.

The rich, elemental hues—chosen in consultation with a feng shui expert—evoke nature: a tranquil fern green in the Forest studio, an uplifting azure blue for the Sky studio, a hypnotic terra-cotta in the Earth studio, and an invigorating fiery yellow in the Sun studio. My first class here was held in the Forest room, where I noticed an immediate sense of bodily ease and mental stillness as my gaze drifted up to the smooth textures of the dark green canopy.

While this busy yoga center serves as many as 2,500 people a week in more than 100 classes, the 11,500-square-foot space doesn't feel overrun. I have experienced a pleasant community feeling at OM, with a knowledgeable staff that is genuinely friendly and eager to guide me through yoga's transformational possibilities. I have come to value the gentle, stress-reducing benefits of my twice-weekly, vinyasa-style yoga classes. I'm no yogi yet, but at OM they are very patient.

*Yoga Lover's Note: I have also found a soothing atmosphere and sincere, focused instruction at **Laughing Lotus Yoga** (59 West 19th St., 212-414-2903), **Levitate Yoga** (780 Eighth Ave., 212-974-2288), **Kundalini Yoga** (873 Broadway, 212-982-5959), and the venerable **Integral Yoga** (227 West 13th St., 866-542-3254).*

Open Center
Meditation Room

Address: 83 Spring St., bet. Broadway and
Crosby St.
Phone: (212) 219-2527
Hours: Daily, 10 A.M. to 10 P.M.
Admission: Free
Subway: N, R to Prince St.; 6 to Spring St.
Bus: M1, 6 (Broadway) to Spring St.
Website: www.opencenter.org

Whether you meditate daily, or wouldn't know a mantra if someone snuck up and whispered "om" in your ear, there is something to be said for an organization that earmarks valuable square footage to serve your inner state of being.

The New York Open Center, which claims to be the largest urban holistic center in the world, offers hundreds of fascinating courses for exploring consciousness, creativity, and spirit. People of all ages have found a supportive and healing environment here. And while the Open Center holds many soul-sustaining attractions, my favorite is on the second floor, where you'll find a silent room dedicated exclusively to walk-in, private meditation (simply sign in at the front desk).

The incense-laden peace of this space has been enhanced by the blessing of an esteemed Tibetan lama. Also take note of the mottled rose- and lilac-colored walls, the work of architectural painter John Stolfo, who was commissioned by the center to apply his "Lazure" painting technique (based on the teachings of Rudolf Steiner) to the room: using natural-pigment, nontoxic paints combined with essential healing oils, Stolfo created rhythmic patterns on the walls intended to help meditators achieve a deeper contemplative experience. I've serenity-sampled the room both before and after the mood-altering paint job and was impressed by the subtle difference.

The Open Center's meditation room offers a comforting place to withdraw from a demanding day and pause for a moment's reflection. Be sure to stop by the bookstore, where you'll find a unique collection of holistic and spiritual books, mind-centering CDs, and accessories for your home altar.

Paley Park

Address: 53rd St. bet. Fifth and Madison Aves.
Hours: Monday through Saturday, 8 A.M. to
7:45 P.M. (closed January)
Admission: Free
Subway: E or F to Fifth Ave./53rd St.
Bus: M1, 2, 3, 4 (Fifth and Madison Aves.)
to 53rd St.

I hate to admit it, but sometimes I discover a delightful pocket of city calm and I don't want to share it. I just want to keep it to myself.

Paley Park is such a place.

This is not a park by suburban standards, but in Midtown Manhattan you take whatever refuge you can get. An almost invisible oasis, Paley Park is situated in a concrete canyon sandwiched between two office buildings, complete with a cascading 25-foot waterfall. Designed so that visitors must step away from the continuity of the street line to enter the park, its offering of serenity is most fully appreciated as you walk past the potted junipers and approach the dominating waterfall.

Sitting on the stone steps facing the falls, virtually all city sounds are muted by the resonant rumbling of the cascade. Add the visual play of the water and you have an experience that is both refreshing and deeply soothing.

The small, lighted niches on each side of the water curtain are particularly secluded. A cooling mist bubbles up from the narrow catchment and, for me, nestling here enhances the sense of ease.

Noontime Note: This happy parklet contains a concession stand and moveable seating, which lures local businesspeople and their bagged lunches. Between noon and 2 P.M. on nice days, it tends to get crowded, although not necessarily unpleasant. But skip those hours to avoid a busy midday scene.

The Paramount Hotel Lobby

Address: 235 West 46th St., bet. Broadway
and Eighth Ave.
Phone: (212) 764-5500
Hours: Daily, 24 hours
Admission: Free
Subway: A, C, E, 1, N, R to 42nd St.
Bus: M10 (Seventh and Eighth Aves.)
to 42nd St.
Website: www.nycparamount.com

technically, hotel lobbies are not in the public domain, since they exist explicitly for the comfort and service of their guests. But in practice, anyone who has spent time in this city can tell you of a favorite hotel lobby where he or she goes to meet friends or business associates, use the "facilities," gather thoughts before an important meeting, or even cop some quick relief from a city that can get in one's face.

Hotel lobbies often can be quieter and more comfortable than the best public atriums, and easier to find. Unless you are a particularly wacky dresser, or drag all your worldly possessions around in a grocery cart, you will not be tossed out onto the curb.

For me, the lobby of one boutique hotel stands above the rest: the Paramount. This fanciful space designed by Philippe Starck is not only cool, but also generally calm. I love the boldly colored, eclectic armchairs, the gray Venetian walls, the dramatic lighting on the sweeping staircase, and the overhanging mezzanine restaurant. The bathroom is always open, too.

I also duck into these other hotel lobbies for refuge from time to time, and no one has ever called the gendarmes: the **Grand Hyatt** (42nd St. and Lexington Ave.) offers a quick escape from the noisy netherworld of Grand Central Terminal; the upscale **Four Seasons Hotel** (57th St. between Park and Madison Aves.) and the **New York Hilton** (Sixth Ave. between 53rd and 54th Sts.) offer both anonymity and elegant seating.

The Pier at Riverside South

Address: Near 68th St. in Riverside Park;
enter at 72nd St.
Phone: (800) 201-PARK
Hours: Daily, dawn to dusk
Admission: Free
Subway: 1 to 72nd St., walk five minutes
southwest
Bus: M5, M104 to 72nd St.

this waterside park seemed an inspired idea from the outset; I eagerly anticipated the end result during the many months crews spent reinforcing the old maritime wharf, capping it with concrete, and laying down the circular shapes and swirling, whimsical brickwork that would form today's recreation-friendly site.

This pier is one of the many highlights of the twenty-one-and-a-half-acre Riverside South waterfront development that has returned miles of lost and neglected shoreline to the public. Though long from completed, the plans call for a continuous esplanade around Manhattan that will link neighborhoods through an ambitious urban greenway system, with miles of landscaped bike and pedestrian paths.

For the moment, you can content yourself with this alluring jetty that thrusts 150 feet into the river, seeming to place you at the center of the Hudson River shipping lanes. Along the edges of this 40-foot-wide pier you'll find dozens of bolted, wire-mesh stadium seats pleasantly positioned to allow alternating views of the city skyline and unhurried river traffic. The architects showed exceptional sensitivity, an understanding of the romantic promise of the river and the power of whispered sonnets at sunset—most of the seating is in pairs, with plenty of distance between placements. Sweet.

If you find yourself downtown, check out the fine waterfront retreat at the **Christopher Street Pier** (Christopher Street at the Hudson River). On spring and summer nights, this pier and adjacent esplanade are quintessentially tranquil places to speak softly, share secret longings, and hold hands securely.

Poets
House

Address: 72 Spring St., bet. Crosby and
Lafayette Sts., 2nd floor
Phone: (212) 431-7920
Hours: Tuesday through Friday, 11 A.M. to
7 P.M.; Saturday, 11 A.M. to
6 P.M.; closed Sunday
Admission: Free
Subway: N, R to Prince St.; 6 to Spring St.
Bus: M1, 6 (Broadway) to Spring St.
Website: www.poetshouse.org

If we're lucky, poetry enters our lives in early childhood with the reassuring rhymes read to us at bedtime, and then follows us into adulthood, revealing its artful messages in the folds of verse and meter, affirming life by paying homage to our most intimate moments. Poems are fertile places for quiet self-discoveries, a way to open to our souls on our own terms.

One of the most extraordinary depositories of poetry exists at Poets House. This comfortable, noiseless, airy loft is filled with almost fifty thousand volumes of poetry, among the largest collections open to the public in the country. Bathed in sunlight streaming in through several floor-to-ceiling windows, and tastefully furnished with colorfully upholstered reading chairs, Poets House is more a cozy living room than stuffy library.

Of course, the power of poetry is nothing new to the people at Poets House. They've been "well versed" in promoting the value and richness of poetry since 1985, when poets Stanley Kunitz and Elizabeth Kray founded this sanctuary for sonnets and refuge for rhyme. Today, it is an important literary resource center and a meeting place for poets worldwide.

In spring 2008, Poets House will move to a new waterside home at One River Terrace in Battery Park City (check the website for the opening date). In a space double its current size that will include outdoor seating areas, you can read the poetry you love or be inspired to write your own while gazing out the expansive windows overlooking the Hudson. It is the kind of home poetry deserves.

The Quad at Columbia University

Address: 116th St. and Broadway
Hours: Daily, 8 A.M. to 6 P.M.
Admission: Free
Subway: 1 to 116th St.
Bus: M4, M11, M104 (Broadway) to 116th St.

We all know of Columbia University's academic reputation, but were you aware that there's also much to learn about relaxation on Columbia's campus? Here it is possible to leave the tumult of Broadway for the spacious main quad, quickly transferring from the school of urban survival to a restful course on personal revival.

Safely insulated from the busy avenues that surround it, the campus is an epicenter both for academic activity and reclusive repose. There's no need to worry about your age or how you're dressed, either—people will just assume you're a graduate student or an esteemed university professor strolling the quad.

Relaxation 101 is self-taught every day in front of the Low Library, where you can nestle against the easternmost corner of that noble 12-foot wall. It's a warm, windless nook excellent for a crash course in human behavior. Carry a book—cerebral reading is a popular pastime for all who recline on the broad lawns.

You might prefer the smaller, less frequented quad in front of Uris Hall (look for the *Curl* sculpture of twisted black tubes). Or amble through the maze of century-old buildings until you find your own solitary spot. There are dozens of places on this postcard-perfect campus where you can partake of the scholarly atmosphere undisturbed.

I used to take a bagged lunch on Saturdays to the university quad where a friend and I would discuss the state of the world. The campus was always a quiescent place for intellectual and physical renewal. It still gets my highest grade.

Robert F. Wagner Jr. Park

Address: Battery Pl. and West St.
Phone: (212) 416-5300
Hours: Daily, dawn to dusk
Admission: Free
Subway: R to Battery Park; 6 to
Bowling Green; 1 to South Ferry
Bus: M1, 6 (Broadway) to State St.
Website: www.bpcparks.org

good green grass isn't easy to find in New York. I'm talking about the really dense, carpet-thick stuff that's not trampled thin by soccer cleats, littered with cigarette butts, or dotted with dog doo—the kind of lush covering you can lie on, letting your tension seep into the earth.

The best public expanse of green grass in the city is at the spectacular Robert Wagner Park, tucked between the expanded Museum of Jewish Heritage and Battery Park in lower Manhattan. A small but masterfully designed wedge of land jutting into the lower harbor, there is simply no better place to watch passing river traffic while comfortably sprawled over soft turf.

A team of urban horticulturists has transformed acres of landfill here into one of the finest display gardens anywhere in New York. A vibrant palette of perennials and annuals explodes from dozens of carefully organized tree pits and planting beds, all casting sweet perfumes across the manicured lawns. Those flawless lawns are preserved without herbicides and pesticides. In fact, they eschew the use of toxic chemicals here. So feel free to pluck a blade of grass and nibble on it.

I like to ride my bike to Robert Wagner early on a spring or summer morning. I pick a spot on the northern lawn, stare out at the best harbor views in Manhattan, and let the blanket of soft blades under my back turn me warm and wistful. Good green grass—Mother Earth's natural tranquilizer.

St. Luke's Garden

Address: Hudson St. bet. Barrow and
Grove Sts.
Phone: (212) 924-0562
Hours: Monday through Friday, 8 A.M. to
7 P.M.; Saturday and Sunday,
1 P.M. to 4 P.M.
Admission: Free
Subway: 1 to Sheridan Square, walk west
Bus: M10 (Seventh and Eighth Aves.)
to Christopher St.

i grew up in a suburban home with a big backyard. Some of my best childhood memories took place there. When I wasn't playing in my tree house, the backyard was a private place to hide in a daydream or stare at the sky. While I knew a fast-paced world was rushing past my front door, out back, life was easy and innocent and fun.

The garden at St. Luke's is a little like your own backyard in the city. In fact, it actually performs that function officially for several quaint nineteenth-century brownstones that enclose the secret garden on two sides. For years, I'd peer over the high brick wall on Hudson Street, envious of whoever had access to this seemingly private spot. All my peering was pointless: as it turns out, you can easily enter this green oasis by following the footpath running along the parking lot a little west on Barrow Street (the creaky wrought-iron gate on Hudson is often open now, too).

Splendidly concealed behind an ivy-blanketed brick wall, the two-acre garden feels well removed from the activity that surrounds it. The mandalalike design of its stone pathways and the thoughtfully placed magnolia-hidden benches contribute to a sense of "backyard" privacy. St. Luke's Garden is a neat retreat in winter, too, when the ancient brick walls radiate heat, and the lingering foliage shimmers in tones of gray, brown, green, and rust.

St. Patrick's Cathedral

Address: Fifth Ave. bet. 50th and 51st Sts.
Phone: (212) 753-2261
Hours: Daily, 7:30 A.M. to 9:30 P.M.
Admission: Free
Subway: E, F to 53rd St.; B, D, F to
Rockefeller Center
Bus: M1, 2, 3, 4 (Fifth and Madison Aves.)
to 50th St.
Website: www.saintpatrickscathedral.org

What's the first thing people do when entering a church? They lower their voices or become silent. Which is why—despite it being steps off of Fifth Avenue and a destination for three million visitors a year—I can send you to St. Patrick's Cathedral without reservation.

New York has so many magnificent churches, synagogues, and religious centers, all conducive to inner contemplation and quiet, it is difficult to single out just one. But St. Patrick's would certainly have to be counted among the most beautiful, with its twin Gothic spires reaching 330 feet above the street. The cathedral's cavernous interior seats 2,200 people and contains some of the most breathtaking stained glass in the world.

You don't have to be searching for salvation to benefit from the cathedral's ready gift of peace and quiet. With acres of polished wooden pews, there is always an isolated corner in which to escape. I particularly enjoy the altars to saints, which you'll find by walking past the pulpit at the east end of the cathedral. I'm always amazed to find so much stillness and solitude smack in the middle of Manhattan.

If you can't get to St. Patrick's, I think you'll find these spiritual sanctuaries to be equally sustaining: **Grace Church** (Broadway and 10th St.), **Marble Collegiate Church** (Fifth Ave. and 29th St.), **Temple Emanu-El** (Fifth Ave. and 65th St.), and the **Cathedral of St. John the Divine** (West 112th St. and Amsterdam Ave.), which has the additional attraction of live peacocks displaying themselves on the adjacent Pulpit Lawn.

South Cove

Address: South End Ave. at Battery Park City
Hours: Daily, 24 hours
Admission: Free
Subway: A, C, E to World Trade Center,
walk west
Bus: M10 (Eighth Ave.) to Battery Park City
Website: www.bpcparks.org

September 11, 2001, changed the landscape of Manhattan's southern tip forever. But despite great loss and destruction, this riverfront refuge remained intact. And today, even with a massive construction effort underway on the new Freedom Tower nearby, you can find a wealth of waterside peace and quiet here.

Whenever I approach this charming inlet, it reminds me how much and how often I long to be near water. Everything about South Cove—from the boulder-studded boardwalk and bowed bridge to the arching jetty and crownlike observation deck—is designed to get visitors closer to the shoreline. You can see, smell, sometimes even feel the surge of the river from any point along the curving architecture of this sheltered recess. The harmonious sounds of its swirling eddies call you to the water's edge. The three-acre coastal park overflows with sunny seats, too, like the rail-tie benches against the south-facing wall that stay warm even in winter.

The extremely safe, always quiet South Cove reveals its most compelling feature at night, when cobalt-blue ship's lanterns turn the nook into a romantic fantasyland. This is the precious, whispering light of the heart—take along a special friend.

*Traveler's Note: Walk north along the bench-lined esplanade to the **World Financial Center Plaza** where the financial visionaries of Wall Street spent a fortune to create a wharflike mall that is not only spectacular to look at, but is also designed to be a haven for frazzled money managers. It'll work for you, too.*

Strawberry Fields

Address: Central Park West at 72nd St.
Hours: Daily, dawn to dusk
Admission: Free
Subway: B or C to 72nd St.
Bus: M10 (Seventh and Eighth Aves.) to
72nd St.; M72 (72nd St. crosstown) to
Central Park West

In 1981, Strawberry Fields was named a "Garden of Peace" in memory of Beatles icon John Lennon, who enjoyed walking through this section of Central Park with his wife, Yoko Ono, and young son Sean. In the years since, the teardrop-shaped area has lived up to that designation, becoming an essential destination for reverent fans of one of New York's adopted sons.

Located across the street from the Dakota, where Ono still lives, this free-flowing, four-and-a-half-acre living memorial to Lennon seems to be permanently imbued with the spirit of the sixties. Once you step over the black-and-white

"Imagine" mosaic embedded in the footpath leading to Strawberry Fields, you feel just a bit more hopeful—much like we did back then.

The first thing you'll notice about this idyllic setting is that it's scrupulously cared for, thanks to private funds earmarked for its upkeep. Sun-dappled and friendly in every season, the planted flowerbeds and grassy knolls get daily, almost constant attention. Strawberry Fields is also marked as a "Quiet Zone." While New Yorkers can be less than fanatical in their observance of these posted notices, respect for Lennon does appear to mute the activities of both tourists and residents who visit.

You won't have any trouble finding breathing space here, but you can treat yourself to a particularly restorative experience by walking to the northern-most end of the upper lawn where it comes to an abrupt point. See that handsome redwood tree in front of the hedge line? Under that tree I fed a sparrow a piece of bread from my hand. Imagine.

Sutton Place Park

Address: Sutton Place at 57th St.
Hours: Daily, dawn to dusk
Admission: Free
Subway: 4, 5, 6 to 59th St., walk east
Bus: M15 (First and Second Aves.) to 57th St.

the most rejuvenating urban parks are those with a distinct feeling of detachment from the noise and turbulence of the city.

The physical design of Sutton Place Park makes it just such a hospitable setting. A 3-foot retaining wall and an 8-foot drop from street level completely conceal this park from Sutton Place and 57th Street. But it's there, tucked between a stately brownstone and a tall residential building. Descend the switchback ramp and you'll enter a friendly and protected realm.

At first, your gaze settles on *Porcellino*, the lounging, life-size wild boar (a replica of a beloved bronze sculpture in Florence), who patiently and imposingly presides over this quiet quadrangle. Next, your eyes are drawn to the movement of the East River—the park's visual focal point. If you stand near the edge of the park and look out, you have the feeling you're suspended over swirling waters. This evokes the pleasant sensation of riding atop the river currents, and lures the mind away from outer-world intrusions.

Tastefully renovated in 2006, the park has never been more appealing. New additions include walkways designed in a grid pattern of bold, red brick, a granite-rimmed circular sandbox, four grassy play areas, and nineteenth century-style Bishop's Crook lamps. Sutton Place is also one of the city's most exclusive neighborhoods, and as a result, this cribbed quad is well protected. Visitors here are genteel and respectful, the atmosphere is sedate, and you'll ascend the ramp to the real world with renewed equanimity.

The Terrace at 40th Street

Address: 622 Third Ave. at 40th St.
Hours: April 1 to Nov. 1, Monday through
Friday, 7 A.M. to 8 P.M., Saturday and Sunday
9 A.M. to 6 P.M.; Nov. 2 to March 31,
Monday through Friday, 9 A.M. to 6 P.M.;
closed weekends
Admission: Free
Subway: 4, 5, 6, 7 to Grand Central,
walk southeast
Bus: M101 (Third and Lexington Aves.)
to 40th St.

Iike most people who pass under this rooftop terrace, you'll assume it's a private "patio" for the restaurant below, bearing a "customers only" status. In fact, this is a public space designed for your alfresco pleasure.

You can enter this airy terrace—hovering 25 feet above the street—from the steep, outdoor staircase on Third Avenue, just north of 40th Street (if your thighs start burning, there's elevator access in the northwest corner of the building). There are no amenities, and nothing particularly fancy about this hidden setting, just plenty of fixed, mesh-metal benches and a dozen silver lunch tables with movable chairs, all nestled among large concrete planters with tender young birch trees and dense shrubs for privacy. Two trellises at the east and west ends of this sunlit space, both covered with faux grapevines, offer some protection from the sun at high noon. Good security and very few people (perhaps thanks to all those stairs) heighten the "lofty" appeal.

You can enjoy a leisurely, brown-bag lunch here, gather your thoughts before a big meeting, or tilt your head back and gaze into the patch of dizzying sky framed by five office buildings looming above. This induces a delightful state of reverie.

While sounds from Third Avenue can occasionally climb up the walls and spill onto the terrace, I'm still happy to know it's here—an unadorned, yet always reliable escape from the stresses of Midtown.

Tsampa

Address: 212 East 9th St., bet. Second and Third Aves.
Phone: (212) 614-3226
Hours: Open daily, 5 P.M. to 11:30 P.M.
Admission: $8.95–$12.95 for entrees
Subway: 6 to Astor Place; N, R to 8th St., walk east
Bus: M15 (First and Second Aves.) to 9th St.

It's tricky finding a peaceful dining refuge in New York. If it's too quiet, the food is probably below average or, worse, the restaurant is about to shutter its doors. What I look for is a place where management is attentive to ambience and consciously creates an environment where easy conversational tones are possible.

I appreciate the effort they make at Tsampa, where reasonably priced, flavorful Tibetan dishes are served under a prayer flag, the overhead lighting is subdued, and soul-soothing Eastern chants or flute music aids digestion. Ask for a table in the back room, where you can eat and talk without straining your vocal chords as you gaze out at a spotlit, well-loved window garden complete with Buddhas, altarpieces, and vibrant growth. Sipping a cup of Tibetan bocha tea while listening to the trickling water fountain brings an agreeable belly-calming stillness to the end of a happy meal.

A diner's right to relaxed conversation is respected at these eateries, too: **Paola's** (245 East 84th St., 212-794-1890) serves fresh pasta in peace, in a low-key setting; the intimate **Métisse French Bistro** (239 West 105th St., 212-666-8825) has fine food near Columbia University; **Vatan Indian Restaurant** (409 Third Ave., 212-689-5666) offers private booths; **Emilio's Ballato** (55 East Houston St., 212-274-8881) is my favorite for subtle celebrity watching; and **New Leaf Café** (Fort Tryon Park, 212-568-5323) has romantic, open-air dining overlooking the Palisades. Incidentally, I've purposely included only Manhattan restaurants—in Brooklyn, Queens, and the other boroughs, it can be much easier to avoid a high-decibel dinner.

United Nations Garden

Address: First Ave. at 45th St.
Phone: (212) 963-1234
Hours: Daily, 11 A.M. to 3 P.M.
Admission: Free; no food or drink allowed
Subway: 4, 5, 6 to Grand Central, walk east
Bus: M15 (First and Second Aves.) to 42nd St.;
M42 (42nd St. crosstown)
to First Ave.
Website: www.un.org

dismissed as too touristy by most New Yorkers, this monument to global brotherhood offers one of the most reliable destinations for peace and quiet in the city—specifically, the expansive, underutilized garden on the north side of the UN's celebrated glass and concrete Secretariat building.

The UN's new security measures (you'll have to pass through an airportlike screening) are, admittedly, an imposition. But once inside, you'll find many opportunities for alone time within the sixteen acres of grounds and garden. Rows of mature oak and hawthorn trees buffer the walking paths from the traffic on First Avenue. You can rest on strategically placed benches facing evocative antiwar sculptures, or enjoy a half-mile paved esplanade offering spectacular views of the East River. This is truly a walkway of the world, with a mosaic of smiling faces from almost every country assuring you that global peace is still possible.

I always go in springtime, when 1,400 prize-winning rosebushes join almost 200 cherry trees in a jubilant display of color. I also gravitate toward the Eleanor Roosevelt Memorial in the northeast corner of the garden. It's tucked away behind a small stand of trees, and from the seclusion of its huge granite bench you can while away an entire afternoon. Or even doze undisturbed.

Peacenik's Note: If every firearm was as useless as the twisted pistol sculpture near the UN's 45th Street entrance, we could dispense with a lot of that tight security.

Wave Hill

Address: 675 West 252nd St., Bronx
Phone: (718) 549-3200
Hours: Summer, Tuesday through Sunday,
9 A.M. to 5:30 P.M.; Winter, to 4:30 P.M.;
closed Monday
Admission: $4 (free Tuesdays, also free
December through February)
Subway/Bus/Auto: Check website for directions
Website: www.wavehill.org

New Yorkers love to get out of the city, to catch the train or pack a car on Friday afternoons and head off to a country home, beach cottage, or cabin in the woods. But for those of us not lucky enough to own a weekend retreat, is there a way to stay and still get away?

Fret not, for you can enjoy all the pleasures of a country estate at magnificent Wave Hill. Currently owned by the city, the Wave Hill estate in the Riverdale section of the Bronx performs the same function as it did when such famous former residents as Teddy Roosevelt, Mark Twain, and Arturo Toscanini made it their weekend getaway. Today it offers nature-deprived city folk a verdant escape just twenty minutes from Manhattan.

The twenty-eight acres of award-winning gardens, greenhouses, sweeping lawns, huge copper beech trees, a lily pond, and unspoiled woodlands occupy a hilltop that brings you face-to-face with the Palisades—a geologic wonder that never fails to astonish. The former mansion contains a gift shop and café with outdoor seating, as well as a children's arts and environmental-education center. There's also plenty of clean air and open land at Wave Hill, and lots of inviting spots to turn your back on a tight and toxic city. Many gravitate toward the picturesque, rough-hewn gazebo in the Wild Garden, but I'm partial to the high-backed signature lawn chairs generously distributed throughout the grounds.

Bring your watercolors. You might be inspired to paint soothing, soft-hued pictures of your pseudo–country home to hang on your city walls.

Yelo

Address: 315 West 57th St., bet. Eighth and
Ninth Aves.
Phone: (212) 245-8235
Hours: Monday through Friday, 10 A.M. to
9 P.M.; Saturday and Sunday, 12 P.M. to 8 P.M.
Admission: $12 for 20 minutes, $24 for
40 minutes
Subway: N, R to 57th St.; A, E to 59th St.
Bus: M10 (Seventh and Eighth Aves.) to
57th St.
Website: www.yelonyc.com

Yelo had me hooked about two minutes after I
entered my sleek "napping pod" and plunked
myself down on the cozy, custom recliner. The
attendant was describing the features of my private relaxation cabin, but I couldn't concentrate.
I felt so drowsy. I wanted her to stop talking so I
could surrender to my sinking eyelids and doze
off. The weird thing is, it was morning. And I
wasn't tired. And I'm not really a nap person!

What you discover quickly at Yelo, however, is
that this is not your kindergarten-variety nap.
This is high-tech relaxation therapy based on the
latest sleep science, and you'd have to be on a

bushel of amphetamines and a bucket of caffeine not to succumb.

Owner Nic Ronco knows more about the rejuvenating power of napping than the Sandman. He can quote from reams of scientific evidence about the benefits of daily naps, including increased productivity and mental alertness, reduced stress, and improved overall well-being.

The somnolence begins inside his specially designed YeloCabs—virtually soundproof, honeycomb-shaped sleep pods. A soft recliner surrounds you like a beige leather cocoon, elevating your legs for a feeling of weightlessness that slows your heart rate. You customize the colors of the unique LED lighting system to wake you from your slumber with soothing, simulated daylight, and select from a choice of calming music or soporific environmental soundtracks. The effect is magical and immediate—like mainlining melatonin with none of the risks.

It's naptime, New York—at Yelo. Bring your own milk and cookies.

15 More Great Urban Sanctuaries...

because you can
never have enough
peace and quiet.

AIA Center for Architecture

Address: 536 LaGuardia Pl., just north of
Bleecker St.
Phone: (212) 683-0023
Website: www.aiany.org

I like buildings that like people. Buildings designed on a human scale, flooded with natural light so you're not longing to be outside when you're in. The American Institute of Architecture, an elegant and serene gallery where you can immerse yourself in architecture-related events and exhibitions, is exactly this kind of place. Its dramatic 64-foot-wide glass façade is part of an ingenious lighting scheme that ushers luminous, soothing natural light deep into two sub-basement venues. Contributing to the center's tranquil appeal is the conscious attention to sustainability—with renewable cork flooring and wall coverings throughout, plus the first geothermal system in a public building in Manhattan. The result is a pleasing space that invites you to shift effortlessly into a lower gear before re-engaging with the city's quickened pulse.

The Bike Path on the Hudson River Greenway

Address: Battery Park to 207th St.

Pedal strokes are like a cadenced meditation to me. Which is why I have much gratitude to the city for its ongoing commitment to building safe, scenic, traffic-free trails for cyclists (and serenity-seekers) throughout the five boroughs. My favorite stretch serpentines the length of the Hudson River Greenway on the West Side waterfront of Manhattan. While there are plenty of grassy spots to scoot off the path and stretch awhile, the pier parks from Christopher Street to 26th Street are the most inviting. But don't neglect the beautiful northern-most portions of the bikeway, from 140th Street to 207th Street, where the cycling crowds thin out dramatically. There are also great routes in the other boroughs: in Staten Island, pedal the picturesque 4 miles of the FDR Boardwalk; while in Queens, enjoy the amiable bike path that loops lazily around Meadow Lake in Flushing Meadows-Corona Park.

Brooklyn Botanic Garden

Address: 1000 Washington Ave., Brooklyn
Phone: (718) 623-7200
Website: www.bbg.org

Few places offer such a total package of rest and refreshment as the horticulturally varied Brooklyn Botanic Garden. This fifty-two-acre palette of ever-changing color and beauty is as diverse as the many surrounding cultures it serves. Two destinations top my list here. The traditional Japanese Hill-and-Pond Garden is a secluded arcadia, highlighted by a bucolic pond where you can watch the colorful koi loll through still waters. Walk around the pond to the second tier of waterfalls where small grottoes in the rock create a soothing aural tapestry of overlapping echoes. Over at the Fragrance Garden, you're encouraged to rub the leaves of plants both obscure and familiar. On the tips of your fingers, you'll capture hints of lemon and mint, fennel and lavender—dozens of inviting essences that can trigger a lifetime of remembrances.

The Flower Garden at 91st Street

Address: Riverside Park at 91st St.

I cycle much of the year along a route that takes me through Riverside Park along the Hudson, where I always make a brief stop to savor the multiple personalities of this enthusiastically cultivated corner. Planted and maintained by local residents who consider the garden sacred, the fenced flowerbeds —about 100 yards west of Riverside Drive—have a beauty and grandeur that seem to quiet both minds and mouths. From late February through November, there are always roses, white narcissus, lady's mantle, or other well-tended flowers making their delicate statement. The garden is located at the end of a wide esplanade that provides elevated views of the Hudson River, extending to 83rd Street.

I treasure photographs of my father walking along this exact stretch of Riverside Park in the 1940s, proving perhaps that the desire to find peace and quiet is a genetic predisposition.

The Frick Museum

Address: 1 East 70th St., at Fifth Ave.
Phone: (212) 288-0700
Website: www.frickmuseum.org

Like staring at the tropical fish in a home aquarium, watching the sculpted frogs at the Frick does wonders for your nervous system. Upon entering this former mansion of Henry Clay Frick, walk to the fountain in the skylit Garden Court, where you'll see the two frisky amphibians perpetually spouting water at each other. This water play is mesmerizing and immeasurably soothing. Of course, there's more to the Frick than the frogs. In this residential setting, you can view paintings by Velázquez, Van Dyck, El Greco, and Goya. The beauty of Rembrandt's self-portraits alone can act as a welcome balm for jangled nerves. My eternal gripe is that they don't allow access to the alluring outdoor garden. But you can appreciate its serene details through the mansion's windows, then return to those tranquility-inducing amphibians.

Housing Works
Used Bookstore
Café

Address: 126 Crosby St., bet. Houston and Prince Sts.
Phone: (212) 334-3324
Website: www.housingworks.org

It is in places like this that many literary New Yorkers are born: walls lined floor to ceiling with mahogany bookcases; tables overflowing with tempting titles; comfortable chairs nestled in discreet corners where you can read three chapters of a relished novel before deciding to buy it; a relaxed atmosphere where the works of great writers can be lingered over, not rushed through. This second-hand-treasure trove in SoHo (all the titles are donated) is sweeter than the Strand and more intimate than any Barnes & Noble megastore. The balcony is best, lined on both sides with enticing tomes that turn it into a veritable browser's paradise. Housing Works has a conscience, too: Proceeds from sales are used to provide housing, health care, and other services for homeless men and women with AIDS and HIV.

The Jefferson Market Garden

Address: Greenwich Ave. bet. 9th and 10th Sts.
Website: www.jeffersonmarketgarden.org

New Yorkers are inherently thrill-seeking, and tend to glorify intensity and excitement. We want everything bigger and more sensational. But a need for equilibrium that dwells inside us quietly asks that we consider the city on a smaller scale, and take periodic refuge in a simpler New York. The quaint Jefferson Market Garden sits unobtrusively behind a high wrought-iron fence in the shadow of the Gothic spires of the Jefferson Market Library. From May through October (every day except Monday), you can sidestep the city and slip into the garden's unhurried charms. This little haven, resplendent with flourishing color in the growing seasons, is designed to stimulate interest in horticulture and the environment. Just follow the red-brick road that snakes gently through the garden, compose yourself, and remember life's little wonders.

Liz Christy Bowery-Houston Garden

Address: Northeast corner of Houston and Bowery Sts.
Phone: (212) 594-2155
Website: www.lizchristygarden.org

This is one stubborn little community garden, but as long as it insists on hanging in there, I insist on including it in these pages. There are now seven hundred–plus community gardens in the city, but this is the original. In 1973 activist Liz Christy and her resident band of Green Guerillas were the first to successfully reclaim a rubble-strewn lot and return it to a fertile place for growing and gardening. Today volunteers regularly till, weed, and water the sixty beds bursting with vegetables, fruit trees, and fragrant herbs. I am always amazed at how a trio of birch trees and a low ridge of thick wildflowers can buffer the heavy sounds of Houston Street traffic. It's easy to see why locals stop here for quick encounters with nature, whether to gaze at the small pond or pluck grapes from the simple trellis.

Mount Vernon Hotel
Museum and Garden

Address: 421 East 61st St., bet. First and York Aves.
Phone: (212) 838-6878
Website: www.mvhm.org

There aren't many places left in the city where you can step into our colonial past, but this charming museum is a virtual time machine. Constructed in 1799, the former carriage house is one of only seven surviving eighteenth-century buildings in Manhattan that are open to the public. In 1826, it was converted to a fashionable "day hotel" catering to affluent New Yorkers who would escape to the "country" from lower Manhattan for rural walks, fishing, saltwater bathing, and other leisurely pastimes. The museum tour is excellent, but I'm drawn to the backyard garden with its remarkable level of colonial-era serenity. Languish on the simple teak benches amidst the precisely planted flora and colorful perennials, or climb the steps in the garden's northwest corner to a peaceful upper terrace, where there's a natural schist outcropping ideal for sunning.

The **Rubin** Museum of **Art**

Address: 150 West 17th St. at Seventh Ave.
Phone: (212) 620-5000
Website: www.rmanycs.org

The Rubin is not as quiet as I might like due to the steel-and-marble staircase (famously inherited from the space's former incarnation as Barney's) that spirals up through the seven-story gallery space carrying sounds from below. But there is something palpably slow and peaceful about this intimate museum dedicated to Himalayan art. Much of it—from Bhutan, Tibet, Mongolia, Nepal, India, and China—was created in service to indigenous religions, and the spiritual significance impacts the viewer. Sit before the powerful Tsam dance masks, for instance, and you'll sense the reverence with which they were created. In fact, the high concentration of sacred objects here seems to dramatically uplift the spirit. One wall inscription from an esteemed mystic captures the mood precisely: "Flight is within our potential as human beings." Visit the Rubin, and soar for youself.

Shakespeare Garden

**Address: Central Park near
79th St. Transverse**

Nestled into a hillside below the Delacorte Theater in Central Park, where Shakespearean performances rule the summer, this shady, texturally enticing garden plays the role of seductive oasis perfectly. Its tightly coiled flagstone paths serpentine up a short hill to a secluded circle of grass favored by early evening picnickers bound for the theater. But it's the garden itself—overflowing with more than 120 plant varieties, some cultivated from cuttings taken directly from the Bard's own garden in Stratford-upon-Avon—that is most enchanting. There is no way to walk through it quickly—the placement of the spiraling steps and rustic benches almost forbids it. But what's your hurry? Take in the delphiniums, ferns, and delicate poppies, and leave with Shakespeare on your lips: "O, beauty, till now I never knew thee!" (*Henry VIII*).

Shearwater **Sailing**

**Address: North Cove Marina at
World Financial Center
Phone: (212) 619-0885
Website: www.shearwatersailing.com**

Surrounded as we are by concrete and steel in the abysmal gray canyons of Manhattan, we can forget that we're living on an island. And islands sit in the middle of large bodies of water, perfect for sailing. The mariners who own the Shearwater, a vintage 1929 Maine schooner, haven't forgotten. They invite you along as they navigate through lower Hudson Harbor, where you can enjoy heart-stopping views of old Manhattan and the Big Green Lady. Call for reservations from April through October on the relaxing morning or lunchtime sail (about $45 per person/one and a half hours) or for the sunset or moonlight cruises (about $50 per person/two hours). This pristine 82-foot yacht, with its handsome teak decks and billowing sails, will work wonders on your stress, surrounding you with sea spray and serenity during an exhilarating offshore mini-vacation.

Tudor City
Greens

Address: First Ave. and Tudor City Pl., at 42nd St.

Sometimes the energy of Midtown puts a pleasant buzz in my New York bones. Other times, it's just too much—and that's when I climb the forty steps from 42nd Street, withdrawing to the slower "greens" above. I have a fondness for this pair of modest, gated quadrangles that have been sustaining the Tudor City community since the 1920s and asking little in return. The greens straddle both sides of 42nd Street and each has its charms, but I think the best spot is in the north section. Make a right through the gates and take a short stroll toward the small gray apartment building in the northwest corner of the green. There's a bench under a huge rhododendron there that faces a concrete birdbath and is slightly hidden by the wooden potting shed. That's my spot.

But I'll gladly share it.

Washington Mews

Walk slowly. No, slower. As slowly as you'd walk
if you were holding the hand of a two-year-old.
There, that's the perfect pace for strolling this
nineteenth-century cobblestoned alleyway in
Greenwich Village. I live only two blocks from
Washington Mews and never miss a chance to
amble snail-like through this narrow lane, which
bisects a block of two-story structures built as
stables and carriage houses in the 1830s. Nestled
within the campus grid of New York University,
the mews is well patrolled and always safe.
At one time, at least a half-dozen of these
private back streets were open to pedestrians
who wanted to detour off busier thoroughfares
into more peaceful passageways. Now only a few
remain unlocked. Get here while you still can
and, remember, slow down.

The Water Tunnel at 48th Street

Address: 48th to 49th Sts., bet. Sixth and Seventh Aves.

Sometimes you have to slip into the cracks of the city to find a moment of precious privacy. The pass-through plaza between 48th and 50th Streets—with a mesmerizing glass water tunnel as its centerpiece—is a wedge of serenity in Manhattan's tight architecture. For years, I would rush past the narrow opening to this plaza and be surprised by its sudden presence. Now I seek out the slim passageway specifically to walk through the water tunnel—a Plexiglas opening about 15 feet long, with a slate bridge down its middle and water cascading over it from a waterfall above. A walk through the tunnel takes just seconds, but it is calming and pleasant nonetheless.

Children can never pass through it without stopping to look up and stare. The tunnel's light mists will have the same captivating effect on you, bringing out the innocence inside.

Geographic Index

Where Do You Go for Peace and Quiet?

Do you know a serene urban sanctuary, a noise-free
New York neighborhood, or a calm city center that
does not appear in this book? Allan would love to
hear from you about quiet locations you visit in the
five boroughs. Please mail them to Allan Ishac,
c/o Universe Publishing, 300 Park Avenue South,
New York, NY 10010. Or email him directly at
info@findpeaceandquiet.com.

About
the Author

Allan Ishac is a former advertising creative director
who wrote and developed the Telly Award–winning
Hard Hat Harry children's video series. He is also the
author of *New York's 50 Best Places To Take Children*,
and editor of *New York's 50 Best Places to Renew Body,
Mind and Spirit*. Allan lives in Manhattan and seeks
serenity (and laughter) through balloon sculpting.

If you want to communicate with Allan or learn more
about bringing peace and quiet into your life, visit him
at his website: Findpeaceandquiet.com.
(Or as he calls it, the world's first "dot.calm" site).